The N

words by Nigel & Josephine Croser
photographs by Francesco Bozzo

Here is a butterfly.

It is a male.

Here is a butterfly.

It is a female.

They fly.

They mate.

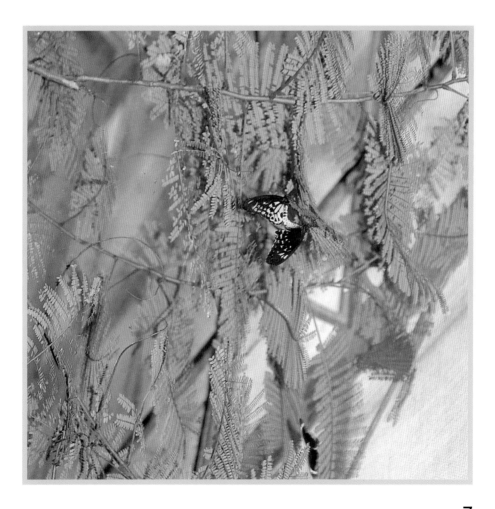

She lays an egg.

A caterpillar comes out.

It eats leaves.

It sheds its skin.

It gets bigger.

It stops eating.

It sticks to a stem.

It is a pupa.

A new butterfly comes out.